Lighthouse
Baptist Church
(508) 548-1692

Calming the Storm

Letting God Help You
in Times of Crisis

CHARLES WILLIAM
STEWART

ABINGDON PRESS
NASHVILLE

CALMING THE STORM
LETTING GOD HELP YOU IN TIMES OF CRISIS

Copyright © 1988 by Abingdon Press

This book is printed on acid-free paper.

Library of Congress Cataloging-in-Publication Data

STEWART, CHARLES WILLIAM.
  Calming the storm.
  Bibliography: P.
  1. Bereavement—Religious aspects—Christianity.
  2. Consolation. I. Title.
BV4905.2.S73   1989   248.8'6   88-8008

ISBN 0-687-04624-6 (alk. paper)

Scripture quotations unless otherwise noted are from the Revised Standard Version of the Bible, copyright 1946, 1952, 1971 by the Division of Christian Education of the National Council of the Churches of Christ in the USA, and used by permission.
Those noted NEB are from The New English Bible. The Delegates of the Oxford University Press and The Syndics of the Cambridge University Press 1961, 1970. Reprinted by permission.
Those noted KJV are from the King James Version of the Bible.

MANUFACTURED BY THE PARTHENON PRESS AT
NASHVILLE, TENNESSEE, UNITED STATES OF AMERICA

CONTENTS

PREFACE

*A*sking why people grieve is like asking why people fall in love. You reach out to someone else in order to complete your own life. When you love another person, it's costly. Whether you are a parent nurturing a child, a sister honoring a brother, a friend cherishing a friend, or a lover sacrificing for a beloved, loving others—*really* loving them—makes you vulnerable to hurt. For you may possibly lose those you love. And when you lose a loved one, you are in pain. That pain is called sorrowing—grief. You fall in love, the relationship breaks up, and you grieve. Why? Because you are human, and human beings love and grieve over the loss of loved ones. It is as simple and as profound as that!

God intends for us to lose as well as to win. In fact, God's world is one where loss often precedes a period of growth and gain. The losses caused by death or separation from a loved one or the loss of a job help an individual discover resources, both inner and outer, and perceive the leading of God into a larger realm. Sorrowing over loss is within the scheme of things. It is written into human experience, no matter how hard persons try to avoid that particular pain. How you work through the normal "sorrow" experiences—how the stress of loss helps you grow—is what I am writing about in this book. I want to show how a person's faith can become a healing resource that helps one acknowledge loss when it happens and helps one become aware of the power of God to comfort, sustain, and heal.

You, the reader, may want to pick up the book and read it straight through. I have deliberately addressed it to you so that you may feel in conversation with me. To make it a dialogue, you may want to raise questions as you go along—questions that reflect your own struggles with the sorrows you are presently experiencing or have experienced in the past. I may deal with those questions later in the writing, so please be patient.

You may not want to read the book straight through. If you do not, you should know that I have written the book in two sections: in the first part I deal with the general theme of loss and its relationship to sorrowing: the losses of person, place, position, or powers, and the necessity to grieve those losses when they happen. I then shall present the grief cycle, helping you develop a better awareness of the signs of sorrowing in yourself or a friend. Then I shall discuss with you the tasks of sorrowing when you lose a loved one by death, including the importance of ritualizing that sorrow. Heavy sorrowing—and its difference from normal sorrowing—is important for you to know about, in case you experience too many sorrows in succession, or have been made vulnerable by earlier unresolved losses. Then I shall speak of particular sorrows: sorrowing after separation and divorce, the sorrows that one experiences when one loses one's home, faces retirement, and is confronted by aging. I shall also discuss special losses you may face, such as the loss of a baby through miscarriage and the loss you experience when someone you love takes his or her life.

Then, I want to help you see how God heals our losses. I shall not engage you in a philosophical or theological argument as to why you should believe in God. I am assuming that you are in some respects a religious person, that you acknowledge a Power greater than yourself, who is over and above you and every mortal being. I shall assume that loss brings you not only up against your own frailty as a human being, but makes you question suffering and its meaning in the order of things. In those respects, I confess that I am, like you, both a believer and a doubter that this is "the best of all possible worlds." However, there are in the traditions of religious people ways of both understanding and bearing suffering, including the experience of loss and subsequent sorrowing.

My faith is grounded in the Judeo–Christian tradition, and I can only speak out of it. However, what I shall say also grows out of a career of helping persons through their sorrows, many of whom were distant from their traditional upbringing or who were nonbelievers in the traditional sense. What I am hoping to do is to help you—the reader—get on the healing side of life, begin again after being struck down by loss, and acknowledge that even when confronting your own death, you need not despair.

Calming the Storm

PART I

SORROWING MEANS LOSING

Winning and Losing

It's hard to say when you begin to understand that loss is a part of life. I believe that for me it began when I was four years old. I let a newborn kitten drop out of my arms. Its head hit the barn floor, and it died immediately. Nothing I could do could bring that kitten's life back. I was not only sad but guilt-stricken, for my sister was present and I knew she would tell my parents what had happened.

Psychologists tell us that the infant first learns about loss when mother leaves the nursery after feeding him or her. And the infant wonders whether she will come back and cries for her return. Mother and child learn to handle that temporary but necessary absence. However, if you grew up with both mother and father in your home, you were able to develop a sense of self by the time you began to talk, and in that safe place felt protected against the terrors of night and the frights of day.

By the time you started to kindergarten, you had played games in which there were two sides, and you could either win or lose. And, particularly if you were a boy, or if your parents let you know how important it was to win, you felt pretty bad about losing a game. You probably not only were embarrassed, but if you made the error that caused your team to lose, or even if you did not, you went home feeling out of sorts that you did not win. A current bumper sticker reads, "It matters not whether you win or lose, until you lose."

Leaving home for kindergarten probably taught you how necessary it was to let go of one set of experiences—being home and comfortable with mother and father—in order to be open to another set of experiences—the world of teacher, classroom, and classmates. Probably you were both happy and sad when that happened. Certainly your parents were sad to think that you were old enough to be away from them for part of a day, and that the teacher would assume a very important part in your life. But they were also happy that you were at the edge of the whole continent of knowledge that would open you up to the vastness of language, mathematics, science, and the arts.

John Bowlby, a British psychiatrist, tells us that children develop into autonomous beings in the experience of separating themselves from loved ones and relating to them as separate selves. They are anxious and fearful that the loss may be permanent. However, in returning to those loved ones and having the joy of reunion with them, children learn that they can grow into a larger orbit. Losing, then, becomes a part of leaving outgrown worlds in order to enter newer larger ones.

How one sees one's world is an important part of this experience. Perhaps you remember as a child having to leave behind your favorite place—a beach or a place at the mountains—in order to return to your home to begin school again. If you saw your world largely in terms of play and imagination and freedom from schedule, you experienced a rude shock when you had to go back to the routine. You now must catch the school bus at 7:30 A.M., go to classes until 3:30 P.M., and then catch the bus again, with your time for play considerably collapsed. Your world now consisted of mathematics and maps and reading assignments. It was much easier to see yourself as a happy-go-lucky player than as a hardworking student. And you probably didn't accept change easily. No one does. But the calendar, or one's parents, or someone in authority generally shakes us up to the necessity of change and to the need to put our life in order. Loss of one way of life is necessary in order to enter another way of life. And in "holding on and letting go" we generally put things in some kind of priority.

To continue the discussion about how one's world goes through a shift, consider how you grew in your understanding of the world as you left one phase of life and entered another. As an infant your world was bounded north, south, east, and west by your nursery and by your parents or nurturing ones. You enlarged your perception of the world as you envisioned persons beyond your parents—grandparents perhaps, or a brother or a sister—who were interested in you and who provided safety and security for you. When you began to play, you probably played alongside those who came to visit you, or whom you visited, and they opened up a larger world to you. By the time you started to school, you knew how to talk and to exchange ideas and feelings about how you saw things. Piaget, the Swiss child psychologist says, "Every child is a little philosopher" who attempts to put things together in a fashion that makes sense to him or her. And that world was a world experienced through the senses and the muscles as one listened and then saw, was rocked and then crawled, walked and then ran through that world.

Erik Erikson says that the infant and child learn through psychosocial experiences and this involves crisis. He means that learning a new thing involves a critical interaction with a person's primary teachers—the parents—and in that crisis the person has to let go of a previously learned pattern in order to learn a new pattern of interaction. So infants let go of their mothers and fathers who have fed and bathed and held them secure, in order to develop a sense of autonomy and self-direction. Children let go of this primary place as they learn that there are priorities in the adult world that preclude them from being the center of things. Children also discover that they must give up to the other parent what they thought was first place in their mother or father's affections. Then, too, the child finds it necessary to share a place with another sibling who either preceded or followed him or her. All of this, along with having to share toys, play spaces, and places in adults' affections with friends, makes a child realize that he or she does not always win, that losing is part of one's experience.

I don't know whether you remember the number of times you cried your eyes out before you went to school. Chances are you don't remember them all. But perhaps you are a person who is parenting a preschooler and, in witnessing your child's cloudbursts of tears, you are brought back to the sadness and temporary grief experiences that are a part of growing up. Sorrowing that comes from losing something you prize forces you to take stock of what you have and of who you are. You learn how to value what is important to you and what is not. You may learn how to begin again and to perceive the world differently from what it was before your loss.

My point is that God has been teaching you from the time you were an infant that losing goes with living. It is one of the essential ways we learn what it means to be a human being. Even before we set out for school, and experienced one of the first major separation experiences from our home and parents, we learned through separation and loss. You were preparing for the major loss you are now experiencing when you handled those early losses and grew through them. The loss you are now experiencing has something to teach you. The big question, then, is not, Why did this happen to me? but How am I going to live through this so I will be open to what it has to teach me?

The Process of Sorrowing

John Bowlby has said, "Loss of a loved person is one of the most intensely painful experiences any human being can suffer. And not only is it painful to experience but it is also painful to witness, if only because we are so impotent to help."[1]

The first thing for you to assess is whether you are sorrowing. You might be aware that something is wrong with you, but not too clear about what this physical and emotional state signifies. How can you correctly understand your condition so as to assess its meaning? Let me give you some questions to ask yourself, so you can understand whether or not you are actually sorrowing. If you are having physical problems, I encourage you to see a medical practitioner, rather than assuming they are only symptoms of grief.

1. Are you experiencing *physical symptoms*? Probably the best checklist of these symptoms was given by the psychiatrist Erich Lindemann. He says that in acute grief you will experience the following:

Sensations of somatic distress occurring in waves lasting from twenty minutes to an hour at a time, a feeling of tightness in the throat, choking with shortness of breath, need for sighing, an empty feeling in the abdomen, lack of muscular power, and an intense subjective distress described as tension or mental pain.[2]

2. Are you having trouble *thinking*? In other words, are you *confused* at times and having difficulty ordering your thoughts? Are you having difficulty *concentrating* when you are reading? Do you have times when you cannot focus on a task? Are you preoccupied with thoughts of loss? Are you concerned about recovering the lost object, position, or person? Do you think you suddenly see your deceased loved one or hear his or her voice or footsteps? Do you sometimes feel that you are

going crazy? Do you go through periods when you don't believe that the loss has happened to you?

3. Are you *behaving* differently than you usually do? Are you having trouble sleeping, either in getting to sleep or in waking early and not being able to fall back to sleep? Are you not eating as you usually do? That is, are you skipping meals and not getting enough to eat? Or are you snacking all the time and eating too much? Do you find yourself becoming addicted to sedatives or taking alcohol or other drugs to allay the pain you are experiencing? Do you find that you are more absent-minded than usual—forgetting to turn off the stove, forgetting where you parked the car, or losing your house keys? Or are you throwing yourself into many activities that previously you would have skipped? Are you dreaming of the lost person, or situation, or object—either wishing that what was lost were back, or anxious about what the loss portends for your future? Are you avoiding reminders of the loss—the house where your loved one died, the place where you used to work, or the city where you formerly lived? Are you overactive, having difficulty staying in one place? Do you find yourself *pining* for the lost person and searching for the lost object as though this will bring that person or object back to you? Are you crying more than usual at sad moments at movies, or when you hear a certain hymn in church or when you come across a picture or memento that reminds you of the lost person or thing?

4. Do you feel *deeply stressed in body, mind, and spirit*—far beyond anything you have ever experienced before, so that you wonder sometimes if you are losing your mind? Do you question whether you have the

strength to carry on through this particular critical period?

If you answer yes to many of these questions, you are, beyond the shadow of a doubt, sorrowing. These are signs of what any and all of us go through after an acute loss. When you lose a significant person in your life, an important position you have held, or an object that was of high value to you, you can expect to sorrow. You wouldn't be human if you did not grieve such losses.

What you need to know is *how* to go through such sorrow. Isn't that what I promised to talk about in the last section? Yes, it is, and the research studies on loss, grief, and sorrowing help you and me understand the normal process of experiencing sorrow.

The Four Tasks of Sorrowing

Grief, or mourning, has been called *work* by Freud, Lindemann, and other psychiatrists, and you may understand it that way. It is not play, but heavy and serious work. Most of us would like to skip the grief work, because it is painful. If you pretend away your grief, however, you will only make it worse. You need to face these tasks.

1. The first task of sorrowing is to accept the reality of the loss. That is incredibly difficult to do. Your first reaction is *shock* and *disbelief*. Even if you have been standing by the deathbed of a loved one, when that person breathes his or her last breath, you do not want to believe the loved one is gone. For a day or two or even a week, you may walk around in a daze and be too shocked to believe that your loved one has died. Colin

Murray Parkes says you may get involved in a "searching" kind of behavior, going from room to room looking for the lost person, much like you would do if you lost a wallet or a prized possession. This restlessness and anxiety about the separation is natural and normal. However, after a week or so, you should begin to accept the reality of the loss. The attachment or bond with the loved one is broken; your meaningful activity and routine involving him or her is changed, and there is no avoiding it. That is not to say that you will not attempt to deny the loss, particularly if you were involved in denying the fact that your loved one was approaching death, or if the loss was sudden or unexpected. You cannot deny the significance of the person to you and say, "It doesn't really matter to me," and put up a good front to everyone. Or, you cannot deny the facts of the relationship, make a plaster saint of him or her, and refuse to see that person as he or she really was. It is necessary to accept *the fact of loss.*

2. The second task you face in sorrowing is to experience the *pain of grief.* Erich Lindemann, in his early research, thought that you should work through the pain of grieving in six weeks or so. Colin Murray Parkes and other contemporary researchers of grief say it takes six months to a year. In the first stages you will be particularly disorganized and probably will find that your usual ways of coping with problems are not working. In the early phases, you may be overactive. Parkes says, "The bereaved person continues to act, in many ways, as if the lost person were still recoverable and to worry about the loss by going over it in his mind."[3]

You may want to be left alone, and so you isolate

yourself from others. You may skip meals and sleep. In fact, you may not follow much of a routine at all, even though formerly you thought of yourself as a fairly disciplined person. Without the loved one at your side you feel slowed down, confused, and uncertain as to how to tackle the many tasks confronting you.

Rather than feeling the pain, you now may want to avoid the pain and dull its insistent voice. You may find yourself drinking more than one glass of wine at meals, or taking more than one sleeping pill. Flight from pain is normal, for none of us wants to experience the stabbing, continuous, ragged edge of emotion that loss brings to the fore. You may have anticipated some of these feelings: being terribly sad about the loss that you were to face. Or you may have kept yourself going, particularly if you had a long period of constant caring for the dying one. Now you have trouble confronting the feelings coming to consciousness, particularly the despair and depressive feelings.

Facing these feelings is essential. This is "unfinished business" (Fritz Perls), and this task will be remembered until it is finished. If you don't grieve now, you will have grieving to do later.

As Shakespeare said in *Macbeth:* "Give sorrow words: the grief that does not speak/Whispers the o'er-fraught heart and bids it break" (Act 4, Scene 3).

3. The third task of sorrowing is to adjust to an environment where the lost person, or position, or object is gone. You do that by stages; it doesn't happen all at once. When you acknowledge that the loss is real and that, though painful, you will face into the future without the person whom you loved so deeply, you can

begin to share that fact with someone else. You are sorry for yourself, angry at those around you, guilty at all the unfinished tasks you have let go. You have letters to answer and people to thank but you don't feel up to it. It's too easy to sleep away the weekends, to let the housework go, and feel ground down by the "everyday-ness" of your life. You feel helpless since your partner has died. Or you feel out of things since you lost your job and fearful that you'll not get another position at the same level. Or you feel a stranger in a new community to which you have moved. Or you feel unable to face the world after your separation and divorce. Let me speak to you as though your loved one has died.

You have probably been ambivalent about the person you lost. Freud pointed out that we have mixed feelings about those persons whom we love. There are times when we don't love them at all but hate their guts. You may have trouble admitting these feelings and may project your angry feelings on other people: the doctor who attended your family member, the relative who did not help you during the long illness before death, even the minister who failed to call at the hospital often enough, or who mispronounced your loved one's name at the funeral. Chances are you have angry feelings for the deceased, even such a crazy thought as "Why did he have to die and leave me when we are at retirement age and just when we could have enjoyed each other for the 'leisure' years?"

4. The fourth task of mourning is to withdraw the emotional energy you have invested in the loved person, position, or object, and to invest it in another person, position, or object. This is what Freud called

decathexis and *recathexis*. It involves moving from the disorganized phase to the reorganized phase of sorrowing. This will take the rest of the year following the loss experience. If you have a person to talk with during this phase, you will find it helpful to ventilate the deep feelings you have, your anguish, and your anxiety about yourself and your loss. The pain is extinguished in the memories you have about the loss as you talk about them with a friend or professional person. You image yourself living without the lost one and getting used to the nèw position (and new environment) that you confront without that significant person. You put the memories of the loved person away in a memory box so they no longer haunt you, and you get used to what it means to live *alone*.

But you recognize now that losing that individual has left a gaping hole in your life. You are not only sorrowing, but you are lonely and need companionship. *Recathexis,* Freud says, involves investing emotional energy in another person, position, or object. Your task is not complete, as long as you remain isolated and fearful of loving another or getting involved in the community. You should not be in a big hurry to do this. Some persons in the early weeks after a loss, jump into a new relationship too quickly and do not go through the normal process of grieving the lost one. It is better to wait about six months to a year, when the wounds of sorrowing have healed to some extent and when you are seeing things more clearly.

You take stock of your life and begin to cope with the changes and challenges of an environment without the loved person. You come to terms with your new place or position and find a new context for the life tasks that confront you. How long this takes depends a great deal on the individual and the nature of the loss. We'll be examining several losses in the pages ahead. However, it is not amiss to assume that it will take a year after the death of a significant person for you to begin feeling like yourself again.

You will learn to adapt, most surely, in spite of the loss you have experienced. And you will, sometime within a year, notice that you are coming out of sorrowing and feeling some moments of joy.

Colin Murray Parkes says:

Making a new start means learning new solutions and finding new ways to predict and control happenings within the life-space. It also means seeking a fresh place in the hierarchy, reassessing one's powers and possessions, and finding out how one is viewed by the rest of the world.[4]

The feelings of loss will become less as you pray about them, write your thoughts in a journal, or talk about them with a friend. The crisis of sorrow is then not something to be gone through alone, although no one except God knows the depth of pain you feel.

Finally, let me give you some steps to follow:

1. Find someone close to you with whom you can talk about the loss. If you are grieving the death of a friend or family member, your priest, pastor, or rabbi is a good person to seek out. If you are grieving over the breakup of a marriage or close friendship, a support group such as Parents Without Partners may be the direction to turn. Grief recovery groups are often available within counseling centers and hospices.

2. Speak of the events of loss. If you have lost someone through death, go over, with your listening helper, the things that happened in your life together before the person died. Speak of the feelings surrounding the loss: guilt, helplessness, betrayal, and so on. Direct your anger outward toward something or someone outside yourself. Give yourself the freedom to be sad and alone for a while.

3. After you have sorrowed for a period, begin to make decisions independent of the lost person. If you are recently divorced, you may have to make some decisions before you feel ready to make them. Learn—perhaps with the help of a counselor—new coping and decision-making skills.

4. Wait for light to break forth. If you have developed a prayer life, you know that this is necessary in prayer and that God's direction comes sometimes indirectly. It takes spiritual discernment to understand what God's will is for you and yours. After a major loss, that waiting means not jumping into important life changes as remarriage, a job change, or the adoption of children until you have time to assess just where you are.

5. In time, reach out to make new friends, to become part of new groups, to search for new activities and/or to assume responsibilities in the church, community service group, sports team, or club to which you already belong.

6. Understand that you will have both growth experiences and setbacks and that what you are experiencing is normal. It takes time for the wounds of a loss or a ruptured relationship to heal. You should know that holidays will be hard, as well as the anniversary of

the death. That's why living through the year after a major loss will be an uneven, jagged, and difficult time for you.

7. Be prepared to be misunderstood by family members and friends. Particularly this is true of those who have managed loss in a way different from you: they are happy-go-lucky and cannot understand why you are moody and blue; they keep a stiff upper lip in adversity and do not understand that you fall apart. You will find someone, if you look, who is willing to listen and let you be you.

8. Make ritual and ceremony a part of your life. I shall discuss the funeral below, but now be assured that the more meaningful activities become a regular part of your days, the better off you will be during your active sorrowing. Keep a journal and review the progress you make. Keep the poems you write in sadness, and, when the clouds lift, write something that expresses the joy of renewal and resurrection you experience.

The Funeral/Memorial Service

The funeral fulfills both a public and private purpose for the sorrowing person. If you are a part of a church or synagogue, you probably have been visited by the congregational leader and members of the congregation during the final days of the deceased. Or, if it was an accidental death, you no doubt heard from the pastor, priest, or rabbi immediately or soon after the death. However, there are many persons who are not actively related to a religious group and their contact with the religious leader may be through the funeral director. Or, sometimes persons choose to ritualize the death in a memorial service with no religious aspects at all. However it is done, the private wounds of sorrowing need to be acknowledged publicly.

Within the church or synagogue, ritual marks significant transition points in the individual, family, and group's life. Marriage, birth, and rite of passage from adolescence to adulthood are all marked by religious ceremony. Ritual brings family and community together at times of harvest and at times of planting in rural areas; in cities, rituals mark the beginning of a new work year (now more in September than January in the northern hemisphere; though in the southern hemisphere, the new calendar year may mark a significant transition point in work life).

Within the Christian Church, festivals are more linked to the birth of Jesus Christ (Christmas); his life and passion (Lent) and his resurrection (Easter); and the birth of the church (Pentecost). Loss and recovery from loss are viewed for the believer within the context of the Christian story. So, too, for the Jew, the loss is acknowledged publicly, and the sorrowing person mourns for the lost person publicly at weekly service for a year. Each season with its high holy days (Yom Kippur, Hanukkah, and Passover) is celebrated in the synagogue with a supportive group where an individual's story is bound up in its collective story.

John Donne, the seventeenth-century Anglican preacher-poet, wrote:

No man is an island, entire of itself; every man is a piece of the continent, a part of the main. If a clod be washed away by the sea, Europe is the less, as well as if a promontory were, as well as if a manor of thy friend's or of thine own were: any man's death diminishes me, because I am involved in mankind, and therefore never send to know for whom the bell tolls; it tolls for thee.

When a person dies, we must acknowledge publicly that this person mattered, and that our loss tears the fabric of our social life. Although you may have been the person closest to the deceased, other people were also close and want to acknowledge the loss.

In my years of ministry, I participated in only one funeral where the mortician and I were the only ones present. But he knew the deceased and, though the man was a derelict in the community and died without family or close friends, he and I publicly acknowledged his death. Paul Irion says, "The funeral, coming as the climax to the experiences which immediately follow death, is designed to bring to a focus the experiences and feelings" of loss, that "a life's record is being closed."[5]

The funeral is a place for memorializing the person whose life has been lost. Such memorializing has gone on since the beginning of the human story, and its importance is being recognized in the contemporary funeral. A place is provided for a member of the family and/or a friend or friends to say a word of appreciation for the deceased. As a grieving person, you may not be able to do this publicly yourself, and that's all right. However, you may want to say something before the family, or before some close friends, about what this person has meant to you. This may be tearful, but it is a time when your family and friends openly grieve, and you become aware of the "everlasting arms" (Deut. 33:27) bearing you up.

More than any other event, the funeral makes you and the entire community aware of mortality and the need to order your life before death's knell. God, the creator and sustainer of the universe, is before our time and will continue after our time and sustains us in the midst of our brief time. The funeral should enable you to relate to God in such a way that you can draw on the rich resources of Scripture and prayers and final commitment ceremonies.

Ritual enables you to shape your final good-byes into ceremony. If you have a religious leader, he or she can help you with the service and will arrange the details in the way that you want. Some persons, before their death, make requests for what they want at the memorial, so that you already have some thought about how to proceed. The service may take place in a church or synagogue or chapel; many today are arranging a private interment or cremation of the body, to be followed by a public memorial. Laws concerning disposition of the body vary, depending on the country in which you reside, or, in the United States, the state in which you have your residence. You will need to decide how you want to take care of the deceased, probably before your family member dies. Today, some persons in memorial societies and other places make plans for the disposition of their bodies and/or donate body parts to medical schools and eye and organ banks. Sometime later the medical school may contact the family to ask what to do with the loved one's remains. The family needs to be prepared for this decision. At the time of death, you are in too stressful a situation to make those decisions. Therefore, these decisions are best made beforehand. Your religious leader, or someone in a memorial society, can help you with useful information before your loved one dies.

Heavy Sorrowing

What happens when you are not able to recover from an intense loss? Or what happens to you when one loss after another hits you? Personal and family tragedies appear to come in bunches. Murray Bowen calls this "emotional shock wave within families": a major loss of a strong member of the family in death is followed by one crisis after another in other family members. A teenager has an auto accident; then a couple in the same family announce that they are separating; later, another family member goes to the hospital with a major illness. There is a reason for this "ripple effect," which we shall examine later. But what you and your loved ones are experiencing from a religious point of view is that God does not appear to be attending to your little section of the universe. You feel intense despair, an anguish that does not lift, and a questioning of the very providence of God which, heretofore, had been a bulwark of your faith.

Heavy sorrowing, prolonged grief, complicated grief, and distorted grief are not worked through in the natural way I have described above, but are more difficult to handle. This is not to say that these experiences do not work for good. However, in order to manage heavy sorrowing, you may have to search out the help of a psychotherapist, a grief recovery group that meets with the guidance of a trained grief counselor, or go through a period of convalescence under the care of a physician/psychiatrist away from the stresses life has been dealing you.

What I want to do with you at this point is to look at some questions, particularly if you count yourself a "heavy sorrower," so that you may begin to work toward some way out of your sorrowing and begin to see some light and ways to cope with your troubles.

1. Why has it been hard for you to grieve? Why have you delayed it?

    a) You have been highly reliant upon the lost person. You feel that losing that person has been like losing a limb, like "cutting out your heart."

    b) You have felt both love and resentment, even hatred toward the lost person at times. Now you feel guilty and ashamed for your bad feelings, but you seem unable to do anything about resolving them.

    c) You are not one to give way to your emotions. If you are a man, you have been brought up to be wary of showing your feelings. If you are a woman, you may have shown your feelings openly toward the one you lost, but you feel no one else will understand them.

    d) Circumstances have been such that you have not been able to be certain that the individual is really dead. The relatives of members of the armed forces in Vietnam whose loved ones are still missing in action (MIA) are such persons. If you have broken up with a lover and still have strong feelings for that person and, in your heavy sorrowing, still hope for a reconciliation, you know what I am talking about.

e) You may have experienced one loss after another. Several members of your family died in the same accident, thus you lost several people who were dear to you. That is followed by a falling out with an employer and you lose your job. Now you wonder how you are going to make it alone.

f) You may discover that this loss arouses strong feelings of sorrow that you thought you had resolved earlier but find that you have not. So the normal period of grief is not long enough to work through your sorrow.

g) Your personality has always been shaky in times of crisis and this loss is such a crisis time. In other words, you know that you have a tough time coping and know what any loss does to you (makes you crazy in some way). You know that you don't react as most people do in these times and this period is no exception.

h) You are experiencing a loss that the ordinary person in your congregation finds difficult to talk about. For example, the family member who died took his or her own life. I shall address these special situations later, but you already know that not having someone to listen to you about your loss makes it more difficult to work through your sorrowing.

i) You have never had a strong support group within your family; you have never had close friends with whom to share your emotional experiences; you have never had within your congregation or within the community a personal group where you could be open and struggle through your difficult periods. And you don't have one now.

You now know that you are undergoing *heavy sorrowing*. It's complicated in that it doesn't go away, but sits like a stone on your doorstep. When you awaken in the morning, if you have slept at all, your feelings are still the same: *despair*, a feeling of heaviness and lethargy. After six months you really haven't recovered from the loss and are not able to adjust to the changed circumstances of your life. How is what you are experiencing different from ordinary sorrowing?

In their definition of depression, the writers of DSM-III say:

A full depressive syndrome frequently is a normal reaction to such a loss, with feelings of depression and such associated symptoms as poor appetite, weight loss, and insomnia. However, morbid preoccupation with worthlessness, prolonged and marked functional impairment, and marked psychomotor retardation are uncommon.[6]

2. How is what you are experiencing similar to the sorrowing that other people experience and how is it different?

Perhaps if we drew a diagram that shows the ordinary sorrowing cycle alongside the heavy sorrowing and depression cycle, you would better understand what you are experiencing right now.

The cycle of ordinary grief looks like this:

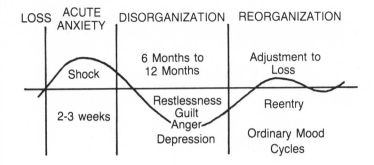

The cycle of heavy sorrowing and depression looks like this:

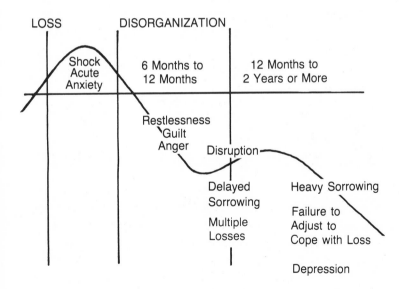

What you need to be aware of is the fact that the sorrowing is continuing longer than you expected, that is, more than a year. You realize, too that it is more intense than you have ever experienced before. You find that it has kept you in the disorganized stage, unable to get your life going again and unable to cope with the day-to-day stresses and strains as you were able to do before the period of grieving began. What can you do now?

3. Is it cowardly or unchristian to ask for help?

No, it is not. You may remember that many people offered you help at the time of the death of your loved one, or at the time of your separation, and you then thought you could work through it alone. Not so! You have not gotten better and it's well to recognize that fact and to swallow your pride and get help. You are probably stressed out, if your sorrowing has gone on for a year or more. You should seek professional help.

Begin first with your physician. A good physical checkup will help you determine what next steps to take. More than likely, your physician will prescribe some medication. Although it is not wise to take self-prescribed sleeping pills during a period of normal grief, you may need some help getting to sleep and managing your depression now. Your physician is equipped to determine that. You should expect that he or she will do two things: (1) make a diagnostic evaluation and examination that could involve various physiological tests and (2) give you a prescription for treatment. This may involve some medication to help your body relax and to help you sleep, and it may include a referral for psychiatric evaluation. If you are to seek psychiatric help, you should see a qualified person who is able to determine the depth of your depression and the steps to be taken to alleviate your pain. Do not be afraid to ask about the background and training of the psychiatric helper and, if you are not satisfied with the individual's qualifications, seek a second opinion, or even a third one.

You may live in an area where psychiatrists are in short supply. Many psychiatrists are concentrated in urban areas; however, there are community health centers for the mentally ill, supplied by psychiatrists from the hospitals in the locality, along with psychiatric social workers, psychologists, and trained hospital chaplains who are available to consult with you. These persons are accustomed to working interprofessionally. If you see a social worker, psychologist, or chaplain, you know that person will be working in consultation with a psychiatrist.

Two resources open to you, which have developed in recent years, are the hospice and the memorial society. Both of these are concerned with care for the dying and have programs for those who are coping with the death of a loved one. The hospices, in particular, have trained bereavement counselors, who work with groups of persons who have suffered recent losses. The memorial societies in some parts of the United States have developed programs of interest to deeply sorrowing persons.

Finally, your pastor, priest, or rabbi who worked with you at the time of your loss can continue to work with you and to help you find the best service in the community.

Is getting such help in opposition to your faith? I would say generally that it is not. Psychiatrists and clergy work together today in their ministrations to persons who are going through loss experiences. The helping person need not be of the same faith group as you—more than likely he or she will remain neutral with respect to your religion or see the ways in which your beliefs work for your recovery rather than for your continuing emotional illness. In many instances, the helping person is someone who comes to his or her task with a commitment to a faith and a practice of that faith. In any case, this professional is concerned in helping you come back to your normal pattern of living so you can be free of the despair and deep sorrowing you feel.

Sorrowing After Separation and Divorce

We have been concentrating on the tragedy of death—the loss of a beloved person and the sorrowing you go through after that loss. What about losing a lover, a marriage partner, a trusted friend? That person continues to live, but is now alienated from you, and you do not see him or her anymore.

"Isn't the sorrow I feel after a broken relationship as intense and as painful as death?" you ask. Well, yes and no. When someone dies, you know that it is final and probably unavoidable. When you break up with a lover, a friend, and particularly with a life-mate, you realize you had some responsibility for the rupture.

Many of those who lose a life-mate in divorce

insulate themselves against the pain by thrusting the blame on the other and trying to act like the "innocent party." If you have been doing that, I would hope you are seeing a marriage counselor as well as getting legal advice, so that you can begin to understand your part in what went wrong. This is not to say that blame is shared 50-50; it's never that simple. When your former spouse deserts you, becomes alcoholic, or physically abuses you, surely you are the "victim," and this adds to your hurt. At any event, I want to talk to you about the sorrowing you are going through.

Let's begin by identifying the feelings you are experiencing after your loss:

A loss of sense of self. This relationship that you had with your spouse, lover, or friend was a bond that made up part of your self. If you were overly dependent on the other person, the breakup seemed to tear you apart, as well it might. You were intimately bound to the other, so much so that he or she represented part of your identity.

A loss of a significant role. You were a wife or husband, which is a socially accepted position in a family and in the community. Others looked on you as John's wife or Mary's husband, and that role does not exist any more. Even Robert's lover or Anne's friend is a significant role known to those in your immediate circle, and when the news of the separation gets out, it changes you in their eyes. Often, too, you lose at least part of that circle of friends you and the other person were a part of.

A sense of shame and guilt at having failed at something in which you had invested a lot. These feelings will always surface, which is to say, they are not dependent on who was to blame for the breakup. You are ashamed and want to hide from the other person's view because you did not measure up to his or her expectations and to your dreams of a perfect relationship. And you are guilty for the part you played, consciously or unconsciously, in the breakup. If you have children within the marriage, your shame and guilt may play itself out in relationship to them.

A sense of anxiety about the future. We are always anxious about something; we fear that something will happen to jeopardize those we love. Now it has happened—the one you loved has left you, and you fear for the future. It *is* cheaper for two persons to live together than in separate households. Whether you are the man or the woman in the situation, you will find the legal costs, the separate maintenance agreement, and child custody (baby-sitters now that one spouse is not available to help with child care) conspiring to make you fearful and unsettled about the future.

Anger, whether directly expressed or just seething under the surface. Chances are it was some emotional blowup that led to the separation, and you continue to be very angry, so much so that the tears are not at your sorrow so much as at your stupidity to put up with verbal or even physical abuse for so long. Your anger may spill out to your children or to your parents or brother or sister, but you know it is meant for your former spouse/lover/friend.

A sense of loneliness and abandonment. This is at the heart of your sorrowing. You were able to satisfy deep emotional needs with your spouse—the sense of companionship, sexual fulfillment, and deep sharing about who you are and what you think and feel. Now that person is gone and you know that, even though he or she is still alive, the relationship is over. It is like a *death*, but the death of a relationship. And though the loss could be recovered, because of your alienation from each other, you know it will not be.

It is not easy to lose a soul-mate!

As adults, we develop best friends who share our secrets, plans, and deep feelings. If they are of the same sex, we usually suppress our sexual behavior. We show closeness to them by our conversation, our attitudes, and our gifts, and by just being ourselves in their presence.

Marriage is certainly a lifelong friendship at its best. However, when you become sexually intimate with a partner, you become less restrained. You unmask yourself—become naked in his or her presence, and want that person to be true to you and you alone. Breaking up that relationship voluntarily may be necessary. Perhaps you have felt that the marriage was poorly constituted in the beginning, or it has deteriorated so badly that both of you are doing emotional and physical damage to each other and to the children, and the battering has to stop. So, now you are living separate lives.

Evaluate yourself as a meaningful person, as mother, father, friend, child of God. Say to yourself, "I matter," *and you do* in the eyes of God and to your friends and family.

How can you best handle the strong sense of loss that you now feel at the breakup of a marriage, a love relationship, a friendship? Let me give you some guidelines. *Recognize that you need a listening ear, perhaps a close friend.* If the breakup is messy, you may need to find a marriage counselor or family therapist. It is best for both you and your spouse to employ a lawyer, a mediation worker, and/or a therapist to help you through this difficult period, before the breakup, during the divorce proceedings, and after the divorce. If you are breaking up with a lover or friend, what I have to say applies to the period after the breakup. But chances are that the separation is indicative that some kind of therapy is needed. I'll leave it to you to seek out that helping person so you may have a "listening ear" and support through this disquieting time.

James Burns, a Boston hospital chaplain, worked with Erich Lindemann in the decade following the Coconut Grove fire. He was aware of how that tragedy precipitated family crises and how working through a divorce is similar to grief work.[7] He pointed out that the divorced person goes through the same shock, disorganization, and reorganization phases that the person goes through when the loved one is lost by death. You are aware that you go through a decided shift from the time when you were fighting for the marriage, with all the problems and conflicts you had with your spouse, to the present when you recognize that the marriage is over. Previously, you may have been wanting *to win,* at least to stand up for your rights and not be "put down" or defeated by your spouse. Now you realize that the fight, at least for the marriage, is over, and you are left with the shambles of things. You may have won a number of concessions from your former mate, but why do you feel so awful inside?

It's hard to lose someone who is still walking around the community. A *New Yorker* cartoon shows a couple looking askance at a single woman who meets them on the street, and says, "Why, Ed Phillips! I haven't seen you since our divorce!" (M. Stevens, *The New Yorker*, October 12, 1987, p. 130). But that's just it: you are alone, and probably he or she is not. In fact there may have been another person in the picture right along, and this has added to your hurt and angry feelings.

Spend some time alone, working through these feelings. You may find old feelings emerging; times when you were rejected before. You remember during sleepless nights the time when you were the last one chosen in intramural sports or when you did not have an escort for the big dance at school. If you are talking with a friend or professional counselor, you will want to relive the happy times and the sad times you had with your partner-friend. As in grief, you take the sting out of the memory by talking about it; then the next time you recall the loss, it will be less painful.

Face the reality that the relationship is over, finished, done with. Continuing to feel sorry for yourself gets you nowhere, and, incidentally, may drive *some* of your present friends away. Now is the time to recognize that the relationship is over. You may continue to see your former mate, particularly if you share child-custody, but no longer as a spouse-companion.

Accept your share of responsibility for the breakup of the relationship. That is hard to do, particularly if the other person took the initiative to seek a separation, or to break up the friendship. This is often too damaging to your slim sense of self during a divorce. But in the weeks and months after the final decree, you need to stop blaming the other person and to recognize the way in which you colluded in bringing about the separation. Every relationship is based on the mutual satisfaction of needs and expectations. Some of yours may have been ungratified needs, which you have been carrying around with you since your growing-up years. Without realizing it, you projected these on your spouse, lover, or friend. And whether you realized it or not, he or she projected earlier ungratified needs upon you. This collusion may have been in balance for a while—while you were "in love," infatuated with each other or deeply involved in your friendship. When one began to disappoint the other in the fulfillment of these needs and expectations, then the relationship began to be in trouble. Your conflicts and angers may have been generated over this kind of trouble. Perhaps each of you has grown in your ideas of what you want to do vocationally, what you want to do with your life at this current stage. What held you together in the early days of the relationship no longer appears to matter so much. One, or maybe both, of you outgrew the relationship. Can you accept your responsibility in these matters and get beyond blaming?

Work through the guilt you feel at having done damage to yourself and to the other and at having broken your promise to God and to your family. This is realistic guilt, for you have broken vows, if you have been married, particularly "to love and to cherish until death do us part." You said those vows at a high moment before the altar of God, and you believed them to be a sacred covenant. You have always said you did not believe in divorce, but here you are involved in a separation, and you are working with a lawyer to sever your marriage. You know that what you have done is sinful, in that it hurts you and your mate, and probably will hurt the children of your marriage. Nonetheless, you could be accepting too much blame and be trying to play both sides of the dialogue, assuming guilt for yourself, your husband or wife, and everyone else in the family. Work this through with the counselor you are consulting, for it may be that you are carrying too much guilt for what has happened.

It is difficult in our society to face up to interpersonal failure and loss. Losing a mate, lover, or friend makes you want to curl up and hide from public view. Nevertheless, people today do not put the letter "D" on a divorced woman, as they put the letter "A" on Hester Prynne in Hawthorne's *Scarlet Letter*. You want permanence in a relationship, and this separation shakes your belief in people and in your expectations of anything being permanent. You may raise these questions with God in your prayer life. You certainly should bring them out into the open, rather than denying them, when you talk with a friend and/or helping person.

When you can, and I believe this is possible through the grace of God, *reach out to the other person who has left you and forgive him or her*. You have heard of God's gracious presence from your childhood, but perhaps you have not had such a radical loss in your life until now. Losing a mate, a lover, a friend is a crisis that shakes you to your boot tops. The gospel says that God is a loving, forgiving presence who ministers to those who acknowledge their need for help. God accepts you as you are with no ifs, ands, or buts. The cross, for Christians, is a symbol of such forgiving love; the resurrection is a symbol that life can begin over again, after the severest loss. You don't have to do anything to deserve this, simply accept God's gracious acceptance. So, begin to walk with your head up, openly aware that this is a new day, conscious of God's gracious support. If you have gone through a "dark night of the soul," acknowledge that God is there in the shadows keeping watch over you.

Look around you at what you have as resources for a new life. Accept your current relationships with your family and try to reconcile with those who have become alienated during the separation and divorce. If you have lost a lover/friend, after a while look around you at the possibility of forming a new friendship. Unfortunately, sometimes those who are divorced feel themselves ostracized within the church. Now, in some churches, there are singles groups for the divorced and those who have lost loved ones through death.

Parents Without Partners is a group for those who have children and need a support group during the weeks and months after a death or divorce. If you are separated or your mate has died, you have emotional needs. You can find companionship with others who have had the same experience as you and understand what you are going through.

My one word of caution is not to get romantically

involved with anyone too soon. The same thing that applies to someone who has broken up with a lover applies to a widow, a widower, or a divorced person. The possibility for a "rebound" in the early months of sorrowing may be an escape from the necessary grief work you need to do. At some point, from six months to a year, you will realize that your needs for affection, sexual expression, and companionship have surfaced again. Neither the PWP group nor the singles group in the church, synagogue, or community may be the best place to look for a long-term friendship. "Where is a better place?" you ask. Sometimes there is someone whom you knew before you married, or sometimes there is a person who has admired you or whom you have admired from afar.

Insofar as friends are concerned, you may discover a friend with mutual interests at work, in pursuing your favorite leisure-time activity, at church, or in doing other volunteer service within the community. However you do it, get back "in touch" with those who have been trying to reach you while you were actively grieving.

Finally, *put your loss experience into some integrated perspective of yourself and the world you live in.* You ask questions similar to those that a sorrowing person asks at the death of a loved one. "What does life mean?" "What have I done to deserve such a blow?" "Is my life fated to experience one loss after another?" My advice is that you raise these questions with your pastor, priest, or rabbi. If possible, get into a Bible study group or personal growth group that is exploring such issues. (A study of the *Book of Job,* or Rabbi Kushner's books, or C. S. Lewis' works will be extremely helpful in tackling questions of the problem of suffering and evil.) I have found C. S. Lewis' book *A Grief Observed* most helpful as a text in study groups, and Arthur Miller's *J.B.* to make a wonderful corollary to reading the *Book of Job* with a group.

Sorrowing the Loss of Place, Position, and Powers

You will, of necessity, experience certain losses as an adult, particularly as you move into the middle and later years of your life. Getting older is much like climbing to a higher part of a mountain where you gain a perspective on your experience and the experience of others whom you have encountered.

My wife and I recently traveled from Queenstown, New Zealand, to Milford Sound, which Rudyard Kipling called the "Eighth Wonder of the World." It certainly was spectacular mountain scenery viewed from the bus window. Then we went out on the Sound by boat, and finally to the Tasman sea, with cold salt water breaking over the prow and icy winds forcing us to go inside the lake cruiser. Then, to cap it all off, we returned to Queenstown in a small plane, flying over the same area, but from the perspective of five thousand feet in the air. We could see all the previous journey we had taken, even see the lake cruiser and the tiny roads through the gorges we had driven through a few hours before. I should add we both were spooked a bit flying so close to the mountains, and having the bottom seem to drop out from under us after flying over a mountain plateau, suddenly finding ourselves over an abyss we had not seen a second before. The plane was small enough to be tossed about by air pockets and wind currents, and this did not do anything to lower our anxiety. However, once on the ground, we both agreed that the perspective of the heights was worth the dry mouths and weak knees we had experienced. Getting older gives one the perspective of the heights. It provides an opportunity to view the journey you have traveled and to see and reflect on the network of people, events, and circumstances previously encountered.

Let's begin by talking about the loss of *place*. A therapist has written that all sickness is ultimately homesickness. You had a place with your mother and father as a baby, and you grew up in a *home,* and whether you can go home again or cannot, you still want to. Homesickness may be striking you as you start off to college, but you have been preparing for it for a long time. You began leaving home when you set off for kindergarten. Robert Kegan tells the story of an eight-year-old boy who decided he was fed up with things at home and decided to run away. He packed his bag under his parents' eyes and as they watched, he crossed the street where he met friends with whom he played until dark. His parents noticed that when the friends went home for supper, he waited in the shadows for a while. Then, with his little bag, the boy began to walk dispiritedly back to the house. The parents wondered what he would say when he came in. He sat down with shame on his face, but they wisely sat down, too, and said nothing. Finally, the family cat ran across the living room. The boy looked up and exclaimed to Mother and Dad, "I see you still have that old cat."[8]

You give up your parents' home when you strike out on your own, whether it is college, your first job, the military service, or wherever. You experience "homesickness" in the separation from your immediate family and long to return. However, you probably notice that you have changed in the time you were away, and that it isn't the same, even though you sleep in your old room and go out with your old friends. It's particularly hard if your parents do not treat you as someone who has gained some independence from them. When you leave home at the time you marry, it is to set up a home of your own. Some young marrieds elect to stay with their parents until they can afford a place of their own. However, you may be one who has decided, as a single person, to put as much distance between yourself and your parents as possible, and, when you marry, you want your mate to distance himself or herself from parents as well.

Let's unpack *how* losing your primary place—where you originally called *home*—affects you and what you can do about it. Moving from place to place is a Western preoccupation and appears to have become a worldwide preoccupation. People move from east to west, from north to south, seeking better opportunities to work and to live. Pulling up roots is often necessary for you to get established in the "right job" and the "right neighborhood," with the best schools and communities in which you and your new family can prosper. Gaining perspective on your life is necessary as you see things from a new place and at a new stage in your journey. There is a time when you can rightly say, "A rolling stone gathers no moss." What you want is flexibility, fluidity, and you are willing to give up the friends you have made and the community in which you have settled in order to move on to something new and more promising.

But there comes a time when you may have gotten tired of moving, with all the loss it incurs, and you want to put down your roots for a long time if possible and settle down in one place. What you want is a structure to your life and your family's life. You want to stay at a position long enough to work yourself up in the organization. Your children want to stay in the same school system with their friends. You want to develop some long-term friendships and to have some things fixed in place that won't come apart or dissolve tomorrow. That is more of the perspective of middle age and the second half of life.

When you reach old age, you still need a *place* which you can call home. You may be at the point of having to sell the residence in which you have lived for quite a while and settling in an apartment or retirement center which you know probably will be your last home. You know you need space for your things—mementos, furniture, and clothing. When that time is at hand, you know how hard it is to let go of much of the stuff you have collected all through the years—children's report cards and art works, things from your parents' and grandparents' homes which you have stored away, and furniture that may be kept for some future use. Separation from these precious things is very difficult, even though a yard sale, which you and some neighbors may have before you move, can be cathartic. The Goodwill Industries and the Salvation Army are also glad to get some of those pieces of furniture and clothing. Of course, all of this is after your children have made their forays into the things and found items they want for their homes and apartments.

My perspective, after having been through this experience recently, is not to strip yourself too bare. Sometimes, in your zeal to live a simpler life-style, you can get carried away, and you may part with many things that you will need in your new apartment or retirement community. You hope to make some place your home until your final days.

The loss of position is also a difficult loss to manage. You learn to manage such losses in your growing-up years. As a child, you probably had a position as room monitor for a while, which you lost to someone else. Teachers know how putting a person in a position gives them status and a sense of importance. Children have had a position in their families as oldest and leader, or youngest and most favored, or middle ones who may have gotten lost in the rush of things. That position may be lost when you leave home, and you seek status and position in the college you attend or the trade you take up. In fact, some of us tend to define ourselves by our position, and we try as best we can to fulfill other people's expectations of us. We have a role and that role becomes important when we explain just who we are. I am a secretary to an IBM vice-president; I am a member of AFL and I work at such and such printing plant; I own the old Hendrick's farm on the east side of town and work it with my family.

When you lose that position, it means you have lost status and a sense of self-worth, if your job helped you define who you are. If you have lost a position, your job loss may have had something to do with your performance. You had a particular group of skills and could perform some task reasonably well. However, you did not develop new skills necessary to your position, or the company was reorganized and someone else who could perform new tasks at the computer or some other new high technology machine was introduced into the office. And so you lose your position.

If you own a farm, production may fall off. Crops fail for several seasons in a row, and you now face the loss of your farm. You must give up the place where your position was assured and now work for someone else in a large agribusiness.

You may lose leadership in a small company to become a member of a large company, where you assume a position down the corporate ladder and feel a loss of status in the move. All of these losses mean a step back, perhaps, from the place and status you formerly occupied. You may be "down but not out," as the boxing circles say. You should be able to live to fight another day.

Retirement is, however, the loss of a position and status that is difficult for many to manage. It is particularly hard for men in their fifties and sixties who have defined themselves by their work. They feel diminished now that they have no place to go from Monday to Friday, or no way to define themselves apart from the workplace. You may feel that way yourself, if you have recently been retired. You have no circle of colleagues to connect with, no task to confirm your confidence, no salary to put a value on your competence, no job description that is a short-hand way of defining who you are.

Some people choose not to retire, but slow down in their commitment to their work and begin to do more of what they want with the time they have before them. You may be one of these persons, who has had a career in the arts or crafts that meant you set your own agenda from the beginning and worked when you wanted and played when you wanted, outside the structure of an organization. If you are a writer, for example, you may be busy with your craft until your final days and never really retire. Wonderful! We shall talk more about creative aging in a moment. For now let's look at creative ways of facing retirement.

You may discover that it is indeed a crisis for you to leave the position you occupied for so long, to clean out your desk and office for the last time, and to start on a new regime. You notice that you don't sleep well for a while, and that you are preoccupied with old hurts and rejections from former days. You go through some real *sorrowing* and are really sick at heart over the fact that you no longer are with the company, school, or agency where you gave so much of your life. What we have said about sorrowing in previous pages holds true for you now. You will need to "let go" of the previous nine-to-five structure that ordered your days. You have forty hours and more a week that you did not previously have to use in any way you want. That can be a precious gift, if you look at it that way.

You will want to develop a new structure, and *take your time doing it*. Many organizations, agencies, and groups will vie for your volunteer time, and, like a person who has lost a loved one or gone through a divorce, you may find you tend to deny your sorrowing by rushing into activity. It's far better to sort out your feelings and then, over the next six months to a year, move through the disorganization you feel and gradually reorganize your days. When I retired I moved out of my office rather quickly in the summer, when I had a son around to help me do it. But it took me well into the fall before I had found the right bookshelves and the time to unpack my books, bring them out of storage, and shelve them. In fact, I had to negotiate this with my spouse, so we found a time when we could do this together, for it was not a one-person job. The advantage of having one study where all my books are located was a little serendipity I had not counted on when I cleaned out the old office.

Many people retire with a lot of fears concerning their economic security. Even with Social Security, Medicare, and other insurance, you might feel you have to continue working beyond your sixties and into your seventies, or to earn extra money through part-time employment, to be more financially secure. What if you were to lose your home or health and need expensive medical treatment? What if you were to lose your next of kin? Would it not be possible to end up penniless and a ward of the state? Of course, anything is possible, but perhaps you are writing the worst possible scenario and failing to recognize how financially secure you are and how you can live, even though modestly, on the retirement monies (pension, investments, and savings) you have. If you have a family, you will realize that those persons love you and will see to your livelihood if you maintain happy relationships with them. In any event, it is not amiss to secure the help of a bank and/or lawyer to help you plan your future financially. If you haven't made a will, you surely will need a lawyer's help to do that. And if you haven't decided about your retirement home or residence, you and your spouse or family member will need to do that.

Retirement gives you the perspective of the mountains or the flight over the mountains. You can find a balance of meaningful work in volunteer service, church, and club, creative outlets in gardening and crafts and hobbies, and leisure-time activity in follow-through sports such as walking, swimming, and various team sports. Chances are, you will live longer than your parents and your grandparents—that is what current statistics are showing. You can understand the losses that go with retirement as fresh opportunities for seeing your life's journey from the perspective of not having to be occupied with full-time employment, meeting deadlines, and others' demands on your time. Your perspective now is seeing one phase of your life completed and looking forward to the months and years ahead when you can, within certain limits, do what you please.

Whether you meet retirement with integrity and a sense of well-being depends to a great extent on how healthy you are. *This leads us to talk about the loss of powers.* From the time you are twenty, you begin to age. Physiologists report that human beings go through a complete change of body cells every seven

years, and that the average human being is pro-
grammed for twelve to fourteen of those seven-year
cycles. Each cycle, however, means that the individual
loses some efficiency of function of the organism,
depending upon that person's heredity, the stress he or
she has been living under, and the manner in which he
or she has coped with that stress. Every individual will
encounter certain illnesses and be involved in accidents that can endanger health and well-being

Robert Butler says your response to the losses you
confront in aging depend on several things: your prior
health before you reach sixty, your work history, your
habits—i.e., taking drugs, smoking heavily, or drinking liquor. The level of income at which you lived most
of your life is an important factor, he says. (The poor
tend to age more quickly and are vulnerable to disease
in ways that the middle and upper classes are not.)
Your attitude toward aging is the significant aspect.
Your sight and your hearing may diminish and you
may notice a slowing of reflex time. *Okay,* so you aren't
as fast as the young men and women swimming laps.
But you have developed endurance and can stay at the
task longer and, overall, you still feel pretty good after
your regular dip. You can, with Simone de Beauvoir,
say, "Old age is the worst of misfortunes because it
mutilates what we have been," or, you can say with
Julia Child in her seventies, "Painting and cooking—
we'll never live long enough to learn the half of it." I opt
for Julia's buoyancy and say with her *bon appétit.*

Judith Viorst, in *Necessary Losses,* points out that
when you age you lose some effectiveness in pro-
cessing new information. You will have memory losses

for recent names and places, but not for long term. I want to return to the place of memory in your faithful response to loss in the next section of the book. My impression, in working with aging persons, is that remembering recent things gives them a lot of trouble at times, but that sitting with them and remembering precious things that happened in the past and friends from long ago makes for wonderful conversation.

The attitude other people take toward the aging is the rub. In a young person's society, where the elderly are not honored for their wisdom but are shunted aside and forgotten by members of their family, you may have a hard time feeling wanted. You may, as Judith Viorst says, feel disparaged as "sexless, useless, powerless, out of the game."[9] But even after retirement, you have a period when you can be fairly active and feel useful at church or club or community.

Robert Butler says that when you are in your early sixties to mid-seventies you are the "young-old," from your mid-seventies to your mid-eighties, you are less active and perhaps more withdrawn and even settled into a retirement community where your health has become a problem to you. After your mid-eighties, you are a part of the "old-old," and recognize that not too many of your contemporaries are still alive.

Losing your powers means facing up to the fact that you are mortal and do not have too many years before life for you is over. We have been confronting our mortality from the time we first knew that human beings die. However, losing your parents, a life mate, and a close friend shakes you and sorrows you because it makes you keenly aware that you are going to die. Not just this shall pass, but *you, too shall pass.* Sorrowing needs a faithful perspective in order for you to meet and accept the fact of your own dying.

Special Losses: Miscarriage, Abortion, Suicide

The loss of a child—your own flesh and blood who dies before you do—is probably the most painful loss of all. What if it happens accidentally—your child dies *in utero* before it is time for its birth? You have been as careful as possible during the pregnancy but you miscarry or the baby is born dead. What if you have some part in the termination of the pregnancy, i.e., abort the fetus? You decide for your health's sake it is not wise to carry the baby to term, and, under a doctor's care, terminate the pregnancy. What if you discover by sonogram or the use of other medical technology that the baby is deformed and cannot live a normal healthy life? Suppose, after consultation, you and your mate decide to abort the fetus? Needless to say, these are not easy questions and they involve ethical as well as religious pondering. What I want to consider with you is the *sorrow* you may feel at the loss of a child you have been planning. And to help you and your partner face up to the fact that grieving over what might have been is as important to face as grieving over what is.

Or, suppose you have a child caught in the toils of despair, and unknown to you, he or she gets deeper and deeper into those feelings. One fateful night, your child takes an overdose of sleeping pills, hangs herself in the basement or leaves the car motor running in a closed garage and kills himself through asphyxiation. How

59

can you possibly live through such a tragedy? Does God forgive you for your part in the tragic events leading up to your child's death? You blame yourself for being blind to the pain and anguish that child has been experiencing. Chances are you have been upset by a divorce, the loss of a job, or the death of parents, and haven't been monitoring that child's life as closely as you might. And you now are ashamed, guilty, and awash in sorrow that you have never experienced before. Are you capable of being a survivor? And is it worthwhile surviving in a world where children have their lives snuffed out before they have a chance to live?

Tough questions! But as President John F. Kennedy once said, "Who said life was easy?" Certainly the Kennedy family have had their share of tragedies. No matter what your politics are, you must admit they survive their losses. And you can, too!

Let's look at each of these special losses in turn. If you are not facing such losses now, you may want to move on to the next section of the book. But some of you may have turned here first. If so, I want to say that this sorrowing is like other sorrowing, and should be confronted as such instead of denied or avoided before it is recognized and worked through.

Miscarriage and Abortion

If you have had a miscarriage or you have fathered an unborn child, you know what a bitter experience it is. You have been pinning your hopes on the baby-to-be. You may even have bought some maternity clothing or set aside a place for a nursery. Now all your hopes and plans are dashed. What could you have done to prevent the miscarriage? The woman thinks, "I might have rested more, not been so active at work, not gone horseback riding or skiing. Maybe that's the reason I lost the fetus." The man thinks, "I should have insisted she take it easy. I could have helped her more with her work. I should have been there when she needed me." Loss such as this hits a couple hard. And if you have tried to have a baby several times only to fail, you may wonder if fate has it in for you.

I expect that if you are a woman, you have been under a physician's care, and that if you are the man you have accepted your financial and emotional responsibility for the care of your spouse/lover during the pregnancy. A physician/obstetrician can help you understand the viability of the fetus and its coming to full term. Now you are having complications that start the body's natural process to miscarry/abort the fetus. Medical technology is available in most urban centers which allow you to monitor the fetus' month-by-month development. Accidents at the time of birth happen less often. However, you may be unfortunate and lose your baby before its life is viable, or it does not survive the birth. How sad you must feel, for the newborn represents the potential person you were hoping for. You may be the parents of a Down syndrome child, or one with severe handicapping conditions—blind, malformed, or with a crippling disease. You may wish, at times, that this child had died at birth. Is that evil of you? How can God allow such imperfection in the world, when all you wanted was a healthy normal baby? You may think, as one mother of a deformed child said, "Life stinks!"

Perhaps instead, you and your spouse/lover did not want this baby. Either you had sexual relations without taking precautions or maybe your contraceptives did not work. The miscarriage seems like a happy accident. You as the woman may breathe a sigh of relief that you are not having a child. You as the man are glad that a baby won't complicate your plans for a career. Isn't it interesting how differently people look at the same event, depending on where they are in life?

Let's suppose, instead, you are the woman and are pregnant and not happy at all to be so. The fetus is healthy enough, but you are caught in circumstances where it is not in the best interests of yourself or your spouse/mate and family to carry the fetus to full term. You are young and unmarried, and don't happen to be in a situation where marriage appears to be a workable option for you at present. Or, you are married, but don't want to have a child at this time and, having thought and prayed about it with your spouse, are agreed that carrying the child to term is not the thing you should do. You have as many children as you and your spouse have planned to have, so that another child presents too many complications in your life. You are middle-aged and your youngest child is in his or her teens. You have learned through the sonogram that the fetus is handicapped or deformed or that bringing the fetus to term endangers your health or perhaps even threatens your life. As you know, legalized abortion is possible.[10]

I shall not decide for you what is the right or wrong decision. You may be Roman Catholic and believe that your church's position presents the right decision for you to make, namely, to bring your child to full term. Or, you may be a conservative Protestant and believe that each fetus has a "right to life." For myself, I believe that the decision should be determined by a couple in consultation with a physician and that finally, the couple should determine whether or not to bear the child. What should you do, given the circumstances in which you find yourself? In a religious context, what is the loving thing to do for yourself, for your spouse, and for the unborn fetus? If you have other children, what is the loving thing to do for them: bring a damaged child or any other child into the home at the present time? What is the loving thing to do for the community: should you bear the child and give it up for adoption to someone who eagerly wants a child and cannot have one? Somewhere there is an answer for you, to bear or not to bear the child. I am saying to you that whether you abort spontaneously or by your decision, you will go through sorrow and pain at the loss of a possible life.

As a woman, you need to spend some time sorrowing the loss of the fetus or child who-was-not-to-be. As a man, you need to spend time with your spouse/lover reliving the lost dreams that you shared while the child was *in utero*. Now those dreams are shattered, and your plans for a baby are broken. You cannot deny the pain you feel. Perhaps the loss led to further complications in the breakup of your relationship or a separation that you did not contemplate. Miscarriage and abortion are crises which sometimes precipitate further losses—shock waves through your whole system. You need to recognize that this has happened to you and attend to it.

Suicide

When one of your loved ones takes his or her own life, that strikes you with special poignancy. You become aware of the delicate balance between the will to live and the will to die. You may have experienced that struggle yourself, and in some dark corner of your soul have harbored a wish to drift into oblivion. But you never thought you or someone close to you would actually kill him or herself. Sorrowing over loss moves some people to the brink when they ask, "What if my whole life doesn't add up to anything? What if it appears that I would be better off dead and would no longer cause people the misery and pain I seem to be causing them? What if I, like Job, stripped of my possessions and health, and left alone, heard my spouse advise me 'curse God and die,' would I think of this as the *only* path open to me, and respond with a cry of defiance against my fate?"

More and more young people are taking their lives each year. In the United States, five thousand suicides of teenagers annually does not reflect the fact that fifteen thousand more will try to take their lives. Drug overdoses, carelessness while driving, including driving while drunk, and abuse of their bodies push many adolescents toward the brink of death. You are also aware that suicidal thinking and attempts at suicide accompany all the losses you and I have been examining. Persons who have not learned to manage loss when it happens in their lives are prone to think of taking their lives. It is an act of desperation by those who feel cornered and who think there is no hope. When it happens to someone close to you, you cannot help wondering what part you may have had bringing it on. You worked with this person and noticed his recent moodiness. You meant to say something, but you were distracted by your own problems. You meant to ask this person to join you for coffee or to go out to dinner or to a movie, but you did not. Then you heard the shocking news that he had taken his life. Whatever possessed him? Why did he do it? Didn't he have enough to live for? Did he have to go that far?

Suicide has always been a tough problem for the faithful person to handle. You probably know the extreme examples in the Bible: Saul in the Old Testament (I Sam. 31:4) and Judas Iscariot in the New Testament (Matt. 27:3-10). It's not that it's cowardly. It's just that with the strong commandment against murder in the Bible, people have thought of it as murdering oneself and, therefore, a breaking of God's law. This is in fact the Roman Catholic position: suicide has long been a mortal sin, although burial of suicides from the church is not uncommon today. Various Protestant groups are now discussing euthanasia and making distinctions between voluntary and involuntary euthanasia. Voluntary euthanasia means a patient takes a lethal drug in the last phases of life after the physician has said that the patient has only a short time to live. The drug dulls the pain and, incidentally, hastens death. Involuntary euthanasia, on the other hand, is not applying heroic means (respirator, kidney machine, breathing machines) to keep the patient alive, when he or she has been told by a physician that death is imminent, or he or she is already brain-dead. These are complex ethical dilemmas which you may face yourself, or may need to face with your spouse, child, or close friend in the final phase of life. Many persons of faith are confronting these questions with more flexibility. Contextually, it is possible to ask, "What is the loving thing to do?" and come to understand that the loving thing to do is not to prolong suffering unto death, but to allow the person to die in peace and with dignity.

Not so, you say, with this person's violent taking of his life! It strikes me as an act of defiance and terrible recrimination against me and mine. More than likely it is. Many people who make a suicidal gesture are crying for help. And they do want you to take notice of how much they are hurting and to stop them from the downward track they are pursuing. But you haven't been alert to the depth of their despair, or to the fact that they actually are planning to take an overdose of drugs and have been hoarding them in their drawer away from your notice.

You, as a person of faith, may think of suicide as wrong for yourself. Right now you believe it is something that is wrong for you. And you believe that given the possibilities that God holds before each one of us, it is better always to let God have the last word, including determining the moment of your death.

Can you now have compassion in your thoughts for the one who took his or her own life?

Can you understand despair so deep that it forces the

suicidal person into a corner where he or she sees that the only way out is death at his or her own hand?

Can you face the stigma that the suicide has created in your mind and, you assume, in the minds of your neighbors and relatives? You want to run away and hide and are extremely ashamed to face others who probably feel you are to blame for not recognizing the fact that your loved one was this close to the brink.

You, as the survivor, feel intense guilt. You feel the dagger of this person's death is pointed at you. The suicidal person was angry at you before it happened, and you now realize that the suicide reveals the terrible rage and hateful feelings you did not know were there. "If only I had . . . " you say over and over, feeling that you could have prevented the suicide by some miraculous rescue.

You probably faced some intense losses yourself before this happened. You may have gone through a divorce, and the custody of your son or daughter was given to your ex-spouse. You have neglected your youngster, or at least did not know that the divorce and separation from you was causing him or her such anguish. You were given a promotion and had to move your family to a new city, and your spouse had to leave cherished friends. You knew that going through menopause caused her some depression, but did not know that the loss of her old friends and work associates would compound her sense of loss. You were forced to put your aging parent into a rest home after your other parent died. You knew that breaking up the old home place caused your dad lots of anguish and that he was having trouble getting over the death of your mother, but you were not aware of how his failing health added to his feelings of despair. In any event, your loved one took his or her life, and you are guilty for what you feel was your part in it.

Face into the reality of what has happened. You have lost a valuable person and the manner of his or her death does not affect the fact that you are sorrowing. You probably have a heightened sense of sorrow, writ large when you think it might not have been.

Acknowledge your own anger at the person who took his or her life. When you are able to do this, you will notice that you will stop blaming yourself so much. You may have been blaming God for letting this happen. However, when you are able to express your angry feelings toward the one who let you down in this way, you probably will also begin to see that neither you, nor God, nor anyone else is responsible entirely for the incident.

Work through the grief cycle with someone close to you—a friend, a pastor, priest, rabbi, or a bereavement counselor. Remember that it will take a year and possibly longer for you to begin to let go of your sorrow. Living with the memory of a suicide is probably one of the hardest adjustments you will ever make.

Find a Grief Recovery Group like Compassionate Friends, St. Francis Society, or a hospice group where others are working through their sorrows You need lots and lots of acceptance and support and permission to tell your story. When others have left you alone, or avoided you because of their own reluctance to speak of the suicide, members of a support group will sustain you as you become a part of them.

Don't be afraid to seek professional help. Sometimes when someone close to you takes his or her life, you go through similar despair, and, as I said to you earlier, you recognize your own struggle with the will to live. Help is as near as your telephone. Speak to your pastor or call a crisis center, if one is near. You have someone who cares, if you just open your eyes and look around.

Be still and know that God is God. The One who is our beginning and our end exists; that is our hope. You may have difficulty believing that in the long darkness you are going through. But if you wait, and be patient, the darkness will lift and light will break through.

PART II

HOW GOD HEALS OUR LOSSES

Looking for Meaning

God does not intend you to be sad. God is present with you through your sorrowing. How do I know that? I know it not as I know that two plus two equals four, but as I know that my wife loves me. I know it by her presence with me, her confidence in me, her tenderness toward me not just in my best moments, but also in my worst. I know it by being with sorrowing people, particularly at the height of their grief, and becoming aware that the two of us are surrounded by the power of God supporting both of us. The mystics speak of the "dark night of the soul," which is the subjective side of the fact that God at times is revealed and at times God is hidden from our eyes. Sorrowing saps our strength and shakes our belief in ourselves, in the meaning of what we are doing, and, yes, even in the justice and love of the Creator-God.

What I want to do is to give you some perspectives on loss from a religious standpoint. There are many perspectives—philosophical, aesthetic, even scientific. What I have to offer is a pastoral perspective. I am not changing hats now, for what I have been saying is, in part, what I have learned from my experiences as a minister/pastoral counselor. However, I am assuming that you have religious longings—a search for meaning and purpose in your life—which preceded the current loss, and which, in crisis, crowds in on your consciousness. Like Job in the Old Testament, you wonder why the individual who tries to live a good life must encounter suffering apparently undeserved. And you may, like Job, ask, "Where is God in all this?" I shall not give you a prescription for some pills to alleviate your suffering. Rather let me again give you some guidelines, from a pastoral perspective, that I trust will help you in your normal struggles to work through sorrowing.

Studying the Scriptures

You might expect a minister to say that! However, I am assuming that as a religious searcher you want to know what others have learned about God in the past and about what wisdom they can share with you today. If you are a Jew, you have the Old Testament which offers you much insight about overcoming sorrow. If you are a Christian, you have additional insight which comes from Jesus, Paul, and the New Testament church. If you are neither Christian nor Jew, you may search the religious writings of another faith group. I shall speak, however, from the Judeo-Christian faith perspective with which I am most familiar.

The biblical faith is a revealed faith and a hopeful faith. Trouble comes to God's people, of that you can be sure. They are cast down, but not forever, for their God is above and in and for the created universe in which they live. God did not create the world and let it run down, as the deists once thought, but God recreates it and works in and through it to sustain it through time. Jews and Christians understand God as revealed in history, particularly in the history of God's people: in the Covenant, in the Exodus, in the prophets, and in a vision of Shalom—an era of peace and justice upon earth. That is an abiding hope when God's people are persecuted for their faith, when enemies threaten and kill loved ones, when it appears that the world as they know it is in the control of the Evil One. It is a faith and a hope in spite of suffering, pain, and sorrow.

When you read the Scriptures, you will find that certain themes recur. The Bible does not question the existence of God, as you may from time to time. But the writers of Scripture do question the will of God. And, as you may be discovering, the biggest question is not *why*? but *how*? How can I, who have believed in God until now, find my way through the sorrowing and pain and travail I am experiencing? And how may I find the healing of God of which the Scriptures speak? What must I do to appropriate the resources that the God of Scripture so amply supplies?

The Scriptures deal with loss, from the first couples' loss of paradise through disobeying God (Gen. 1 and 2) to the New Jerusalem wherein all losses are wiped out in victory and those who are persecuted and die in the

Lord sing, "Hallelujah" as they celebrate eternity around the throne of God (the Revelation of John). You learn how the biblical writers respond to the pain of losing when you read the Scriptures.

The Psalms in particular are helpful to read: Psalm 23, of course, but also other Psalms that move through grief and sorrow to hope and trust in the bounteous support and mercies of God. The Psalmist says:

The Lord is near to the brokenhearted
and saves the crushed in spirit. (Ps. 34:18)
But the Psalmist also cries out, as did Jesus on the
cross:

My God, my God, why hast thou forsaken me
    and art so far from saving me, from heeding
        my groans?

(Ps. 22:1 NEB)

but then he moves with the congregation to say:

Praise him, you who fear the Lord;
    all you sons of Jacob, do him honour;
stand in awe of him, all sons of Israel.
    For he has not scorned the downtrodden,
        nor shrunk in loathing from his plight,
nor hidden his face from him,
but gave heed to him when he cried out.

(Ps. 22:23-24 NEB)

The prophets can be read when you suffer loss, for they spoke for God, sometimes when the people of Israel were in the direst of straits. Jeremiah was one of the more afflicted and melancholy of the seventh-century prophets, yet he could find hope in the worst of times. He could say:

I will turn their mourning into joy,
    I will comfort them, and give them gladness
    for sorrow.

(Jer. 31:13b)

Isaiah also foretold the coming of a time when:

The Lord God will wipe away the tears from every
    face
and remove the reproach of his people from the
    whole earth.
The Lord has spoken.

(Isa. 25:8 NEB)

In the beatitudes Jesus spoke a word of hope to the sorrowing: "Blessed are those who mourn, for they shall be comforted" (Matt. 5:4). The happiness of the saints, Jesus says in several places, does not come by direct search, but is a by-product of doing God's will even in the worst of times.

Perhaps we find in Jesus' parables of loss—the lost coin, the lost sheep, and the lost son—the most encouraging help. Jesus speaks of God as a searching, loving, forgiving presence who does not give up the search for us even when we may have hidden, gotten lost, or forsaken him. God is like the woman who lost the coin and did not rest until she had turned the house upside down and found it; God is like the shepherd who, having brought the other sheep into the sheepfold, goes out into the night to find the lost sheep and does not rest until he brings it back to safety. But most of all, God is like the father of two sons, a prodigal and a stay-at-home. God rejoices at the return of the one who comes back after living a profligate life. But God also wants the stay-at-home to understand his love and care that is always there even when the elder son does not appreciate it and revel in it. Jesus' mother, Mary, who did not understand his leaving home and who lost him in the crowds that followed him as Messiah, finally did understand, after the cross and the resurrection appearances. Through suffering and bereavement—out of the anguish of losing her son—she found him again as her Lord.

Suffering is a part of loss as the Bible understands loss. You are suffering, spiritually as well as emotionally. The meaning of suffering is a golden thread that runs through the Bible. Look for it as you search the Scriptures. I can just hint at it here. But for me, time and again I have found help in the book of Job. The book is written as a play, and the main character, although fictional, represents a new way to look at the suffering of God's people. How does one understand the suffering of a righteous person? Certainly not as the comforters of Job proclaimed, "So much sin, so much suffering." God tends to reward the righteous and punish sinners using an absolute scale of justice, they said. Nor does God chastise each of us in order to make us obey or to purify the sinful behavior out of us. No, God's ways are above our ways, and God's thoughts are above our thoughts. For God answers Job out of the whirlwind, "Where were you when I laid the earth's foundations? . . . the storehouse of the snow?" (Job 38; 39 NEB). Job's vision of God the omnipotent puts

Job in his place, as a human being within the limits of his humanity. He learns to let God be God. "I knew of thee then only by report, but now I see thee with my own eyes" (Job 42:5 NEB). "If he would slay me, I should not hesitate" (Job 13:15*a* NEB). Job questions, but finally trusts God's wisdom in the midst of his suffering. The return of his prosperity is tacked on at the end of the play to satisfy the desire of the audience for a happy ending.

The New Testament shows us Jesus suffering on the cross, not because he deserved to suffer, but because he *chose* to suffer, rather than deny his beliefs. The cry on the cross, "Father, forgive them for they know not what they do," are the words of a suffering Messiah who exemplifies for the believer a suffering God. God does not abandon the sufferer, but suffers with you through the anguish of undeserved persecution. And the witness of the New Testament is that such suffering redeems both the persecuted and the persecutor. Such vicarious suffering is not meaningless, but it reveals the power of God to bring good out of bad, to redeem and save those who are entrenched in their evil ways. The Apostle Paul is an example of such salvation as he bears witness to his conversion on the road to Damascus. His epistles to the first-century churches are attempts to unwrap what his own sufferings for the gospel mean: that God was in Christ reconciling the world unto himself and doing it through the cross (II Cor. 5:19). So you may be crushed down but you are never defeated, for God, as revealed by Christ on the cross, suffers with you.

The God revealed throughout the Bible is a God of

hope. Paul wrote to the Roman church, "We are saved by hope: but hope that is seen is not hope: for what a man seeth, why doth he yet hope for?" (Rom. 8:24 KJV). Hope, Karl Menninger says, is neither expectation nor is it identical with optimism. Both of these attitudes have too much of the wish about them. They have more of the desire to have wishes fulfilled, whereas hope has in it a goal-setting quality. Hope sets goals and inspires confidence in the reaching of goals. The reaching of those goals is not assured. However, the vision is beyond the horizon—that's what keeps the hope-filled person within the struggle.[11]

You may be having a lot of trouble with depression and despair. Getting up in the morning is a problem for you; going to work seems dreary and the days seem long. You will begin to hope again when you begin to set small goals for yourself, and have the pleasure of seeing some small gains. For example, you decide to write thank-you notes to friends and actually do it. That's what I mean. If you are usually a moderately healthy person, even into the later years of life, your body will bounce back from a stressful period, given a little time. Notice that I put some modifiers around my statement. You can wallow in your despair—some people do. But a believing person, even though plagued by loss, realizes that it is possible to set some modest goals and to live by hope; though it appears that all is lost, it is not. As Winston Churchill once said, "Whatever would have happened to humankind, if God had given up on us long ago!" If God has not given up on creation and the possibility to re-create and to renew life, why should you?

From a believer's standpoint, you may be asking about life beyond the grave. Fortunately, we do not live forever with this body. Our bodies and our minds wear out, and we die. Every other living creature—fish, animals, birds, and the microorganisms—dies, too. It appears to be in God's scheme of things. However, as human beings, we long to live forever in some form, to see our loved ones again, and to complete the uncompleted plans and visions we started on earth. Various religions answer this longing for life beyond the grave in different ways: for the Hindu, there is reincarnation; for the Muslim, there is immortality; but for the Judeo-Christian, there is eternal life—that is, life in a spiritual body, not an earthly body. Christians believe in the resurrection from the dead at the end of history; i.e., human history began and it will end within God's plan. At that point, there will be a final judgment, and those who are faithful will be called to their reward; whereas the faithless will fall into an eternal abyss. The resurrection of Jesus Christ is the assurance to which Christians hold, however it is interpreted.

I would hope that you would consult with your spiritual adviser or pastor to help you work through to a discernment of what the resurrection-hope means for you. For me, the words of Paul underscore my faith commitment, "Neither death, nor life, nor angels, nor principalities, nor things present, nor things to come, nor powers, nor height, nor depth, nor anything else in all creation, will be able to separate us from the love of God in Christ Jesus our Lord" (Rom. 8:38-39). The form that one takes after death is, to me, a mystery, but that we are always in God's care—no matter where we are—is my *ultimate hope*.

Beginning to Cope

God did not create you a passive being. From birth to death you live in a body that goes through various changes, growth, maturing, and aging. The loss of one phase of your life journey is the occasion for you to experience something new, and more than likely enrich you in some as yet unknown way. You may reply, "That just isn't so! Losing a baby is something that I will never forget." "Losing my best friend, my lover, my husband is an irreplaceable loss." "Losing my savings, my home, my long-held job are losses that I can never recover." "I don't think I'll ever find anything else to take their place." You have a point there! However, haven't we explored the pain of these losses? Haven't we discussed how acknowledging sorrow, sadness, even despair is important in order for you to work through the stress of the loss? I believe we have also discovered that losing certain persons or things opens you to a new situation where, in time, you will find yourself growing in creative ways. Let's talk about your new situation.

Normally, you cope with the everyday problems you face by confronting them head on. You've learned this method of problem-solving from your school mathematics class and from the test you had to take. You have applied it to the tasks you've been given at work, whether you work in an office, are a carpenter building houses, or are a factory worker with a routine job. The more you manage other people the more you realize that problem-solving involves setting goals, compromising, and using human relations skills in order to attain those goals. If you are married, you are aware that even more human relations skills are necessary to make your marriage grow as you and your life mate seek to cope together with the problems you face.

Loss, however, forces you to use a different coping style. What happens to you is something that you did not strive for as a goal, but it struck you as a bolt out of the blue. The blow—death of a loved one, loss of a position, loss of marriage, and the other losses we have discussed—must be managed differently. Rather than changing the environment in ways that will be satisfactory to you and your group, now you must cope by allowing certain changes to happen within you. You must become a different self, adjusting your outer circumstances to make up for the loss and your inner life to take account of the loss. In order to cope in the second way, you may have to retire to a less crowded spot away from the center of things and allow time to pass before the wounds are healed, the confusion lifted, and your vision of the future clearer. You may learn to cope through keeping a journal during the critical period after the loss and by meditating. You may find yourself praying to discover God's intention for your life and for those for whom you are responsible. You may need to retreat to a favorite haunt—the beach, the mountains, a religious retreat house—where you have the quiet and unhurried hours to begin coping with yourself. A change from the usual busy and demanding schedule you have been under, and a place where clocks, timetables, and meetings don't push you around is what is important. Tuning in to your organ clock—eating when you like, sleeping longer, taking long walks, and being alone—is important to you now.

Pray the serenity prayer and realize that though both coping styles are necessary, now you are seeking *serenity* and *peace of soul:*

Give me the serenity to accept what cannot be changed
Give me the courage to change what can be changed.
The wisdom to know one from the other.

Reinhold Niebuhr

After you have assimilated the loss—therapists now say this process takes six months to a year after a death—begin to reorganize your life. Cope with the loss realistically, with that person no longer part of your life. You miss the lost person and remember the wonderful times you had together. Nothing will ever take those memories away. But now you have memories of the past and not experiences of the present. And when, on occasion, you still lie awake at night and are overcome with sadness, focus your mind on a favorite poem or Bible verse and let its message comfort you. One of the passages that lulls me to sleep during bouts of insomnia is Psalm 139:7-12:

Where can I escape from thy spirit?
    Where can I flee from thy presence?
If I climb up to heaven, thou art there;
if I make my bed in Sheol, again I find thee.
If I take my flight to the frontiers of the morning
    or dwell at the limit of the western sea,
even there thy hand will meet me

and thy right hand will hold me fast.
If I say, 'Surely darkness will steal over me,
  night will close around me,'
darkness is no darkness for thee
  and night is luminous as day;
  to thee both dark and light are one.

(NEB)

The ultimate loss, of course, is *the loss of self*. Losing a loved one, particularly your mother and father, makes you aware that now no generation stands between you and death. There is no buffer against your final end, ever. There is a child in each of us who feels that our parents protect us against any bad thing ever happening to us.

If you never have done it, say to yourself, "There will come a day when I no longer walk upon this earth." The shock of that realization isn't easily faced. Most of us deny our demise—just to get on with living. However, as you get older, the aging of your body keeps reminding you that youth is passing and that life is hastening on. When your children leave home, finally you awaken to the fact that you are at mid-life or older. And at retirement, or at least when you reach three-score years and ten, you are forced to acknowledge that your time on earth is limited. Does your *faith* help you cope with that reality?

Beginning to Recognize Yourself

"Isn't it better to resign myself to the brevity of life and to stop dreaming about immortality?" you ask.

"Should I not acknowledge the fact that my fame is probably limited to what my children, colleagues, and friends remember about me? Should I not recognize that whatever legacy I leave is made up of the few recipes I have collected, or books and mementos I have built into a library, or quilts I have made or pieces of furniture I have put together in my workshop? Maybe I have earned a small place in the history of some institution, or done something in the community that has brought me and my family some honor. Isn't that pretty short-lived? Won't most people forget that I walked on this earth in three or four generations?" Good questions, I say. I ask them myself.

You and I long for immortality. It helps me know that immortality is not what the Judeo-Christian faith promises the faithful. "To be as gods" is the temptation Satan used to tempt the first couple in the garden of Eden, and it still tempts us. It is the temptation of pride that pushes us into believing that we can get along without God, that our successes, our brilliance, our fame ensures us a niche in the pantheon. Jesus resisted such temptation in the desert before beginning his ministry. But it is difficult to do.

I agree with Reinhold Niebuhr that too many Christians have worried about the furniture of heaven and the temperature of hell. That, too, is trying to buy an insurance policy for the life after the grave. Not being anxious about your life is to trust God in the present and to trust God to the very end of your existence. Believing as Jesus did, that "not a sparrow falls except within the economy of God," enables you also to believe "how much more our lives are caught up in the skein of God's care" (transliteration of Matt. 10:29, 31).

Beginning again means to recognize that from what you can understand about God's universe there is both a tearing down and a building up. There is death and there is resurrection from the dead. For a long time I was satisfied with a naturalistic understanding of that fact. Within nature we can see the plants live a season, growing to maturity with seeds in which life is passed on to the next generation. However, you and I are human beings who live within communities that have a heritage of faith. My particular Judeo-Christian heritage has at the center of its faith belief "in the resurrection of the body . . . and in life everlasting," founded on the resurrection of Jesus Christ at the Easter-event. As a Christian *I believe that,* even though I cannot prove it scientifically.

Jesus was a historical person who died on a cross nearly two thousand years ago. He was dead, dead, dead! However, the amazing witness of the disciples—reported in the Gospels and the Acts of the Apostles—is that following his death, they experienced his living presence. They were counseled to meet together, and at Pentecost these formerly frightened, bewildered disciples discovered through their searching of Scriptures what God wanted them to do: to start a fellowship of believers organized around the Easter-event, around baptism of new believers, and around celebration of the Last Supper as a memorial of Jesus' saving power. Resurrection means beginning again, after loss, as a new creature. Resurrection means that you now have the assurance that God does not finally forsake you, but blesses you as a forgiven person and convinces you that your life is whole and within God's ultimate care. Because, as a believer, you identify with Jesus as Lord, the new Adam, you participate in Jesus' victory over sin and death and in the final hope of being with God as a part of God's people. You are today neither dumb beast nor shining angel, but a magnificent child of God. The beatitude you enjoy does not wait until death, but begins in the here and now as you experience the grace that God so richly supplies. The Christian believes that new life continues after the final loss.

Being on the Healing Side of Life

All human beings are either optimists or pessimists, someone said. Perhaps you have been through a period when you did not feel optimistic at all about your existence, particularly if you have experienced one blow after another. Some religious folks take a rather dour outlook, thinking that God means them to suffer. I think that pain, loss, and suffering are a part of things, but that the witness of the Scriptures does not bear out the idea that God means us to be miserable. Rather, it would appear that misery is often the product of our sinful natures, more ready to turn inward in preoccupation with self-pity, self-preservation, and schemes to ensure our power over other persons. God wants us to be blessed and to be a part of a community of love and justice.

People of faith can rightly be called meliorists, i.e.,

those who believe that things can become better, and that to understand and follow God's intention is to be on the healing side of life. It is not a perfect world: mistakes are made by you and by others; sins are committed by persons and groups against other persons and groups. Loss is experienced by everyone and some of those losses appear to be tragic—irreversible. The Scriptures say, however, that there are times when you can expect such losses, and times when you can expect healing to take place, and that it all is in God's good time.

> For everything there is a season, and a time for
>   every matter under heaven:
> a time to be born, and a time to die; . . .
> a time to weep, and a time to laugh;
> a time to mourn, and a time to dance; . . .
> a time to seek, and a time to lose;
> a time to keep, and a time to cast away.
>   (Eccles. 3:1-2*a*, 4, 6)

Things balance out for most individuals, you might say. Perhaps you are going through a fresh loss, and you feel that wise saying is not much comfort. "Some folks appear to get more than their share of pain and sorrow, " you reply in anguish. And you might want to follow Job's wife's counsel and curse God and die.

My experience of the faith is most authentic when I've been able to be on the healing side of existence. I have learned that not only "sleep knits up the raveled sleeve of care," but that God does. "What do you mean by that?" you ask. It's an interpretation of what happened to me in late adolescence when I was ill for a year. I have discovered that out of brokenness, God brings healing. And out of loss, I have had to learn to give up perfectionistic assumptions about myself and to recognize limitations and weaknesses. Most importantly, I discovered that God wants me to be not a *hurter* but a *healer* within the community in which I live. How do I know God is a *who,* a consciousness like me? I don't know that for sure. But I believe God to be that Spirit which is in, under, and between all things, and I have experienced God to be as Jesus demonstrated, a parentlike presence to us.

I would rather die with a faith that moves me toward God and toward loving other human beings than to die bitter, resentful, and alone. Well, you say, we all have to die *alone.* You are right. No one can do our dying for us. But your friends and family surround you now in your loss, and they will surround you when you die—if you stay on the healing, loving side of life. You will be surrounded by the images, memories, and perhaps even the objects that mean most to you, and that should move you toward serenity, acceptance, and peace.

Becoming a Hope-Bearer

Recognize that the healing of your sorrow should give you empathy for those who are themselves grieving over losses. In your most awful moment, think that it could be worse. And usually that is true, things can always get worse. Your lashing out at others, at your would-be helpers, even at existence itself, works against your healing. What I am talking about is not only being on the healing side of life, but becoming a bearer of hope, not despair.

In the film *My Life as a Dog,* a ten-year-old Swedish boy and his brother live in a fatherless home with their mother who is fatally ill with tuberculosis. His sick mother cannot handle the boys and tells them that they must go to live with relatives they do not know. But before going north for the summer, the boy's mother tells him he must send his beloved dog to the pound. But he is a hope-bearer. He hears of children starving in the Sudan and suffering because they do not have shelter from the sun and he says aloud, "Why should I be sad? It could be a lot worse." His resiliency enables him to cope with his troubles. And it opens him to an amazing summer of fun and growth, despite the impending tragedies of his life. As you witness the end of the film, you are sure he is going to be a hope-bearer to others for the rest of his days.

Viktor Frankl once spoke to me of friends in concentration camp who gave up, thinking their capture and imprisonment meant the end of hope and certain death. He said he lost both parents in that camp, but kept himself alive with the hope of writing a book imprinted in his mind and meeting his wife again. Hope made the difference between life and death for him. I am sure that you know persons, who are shut-ins, or deeply handicapped who have no reason to hope but who are nevertheless hope-filled persons. Outward circumstance doesn't necessarily limit persons of that sort; somehow they find spiritual resources to transcend their limitations.

Whether you can become a hope-bearer depends on your having sufficiently worked through your sorrow over the immediate loss, your having learned to cope with that loss, *and your making the necessary adjustments to it*. It is whistling in the dark if you do not start coping. It is denying that you are sorrowing or need to. However, bereavement counselors, ministers of all faiths, and psychotherapists acknowledge that some of the best help for the newly bereaved comes from those who have successfully worked through their own sorrowing.

When you were actively *working* through sorrow, you may have been a part of a bereavement group: Parents Without Partners, Compassionate Friends, Spectrum, Rainbows for All God's Children, Widow to Widows. You may now want to share your support, your healing, and your hope with someone who is freshly sorrowing. Given enough distance from your own sorrow, and having experienced healing yourself, you may want to become a part of a healing mission. Your pain can open you and make you sensitive to another's pain. You simply have to open your eyes to another's suffering. You will find that persons may be waiting expectantly for someone like you to reach out to them. Speak to your pastor for the name of such a healing mission in your area.

Losing and Winning

Like the prophets before him, like many of the central religious figures of history, Jesus said winning, orienting your life toward success as ordinarily understood, can lead to losing what is really important to you. Striving for status and show, seeking popularity and fame, and in particular, acquiring things (building bigger barns, Jesus said, when tonight your soul may be required of you)—that's really losing out. Jesus spoke out also against those religious folk who observe the formalities: go to services, keep the written law, even give a little to charity but harden their hearts and close their eyes to the poor, the blind, the prisoner and the outcast. Jesus said losing and winning are paradoxical:

"He who finds his life will lose it, and he who loses his life for my sake will find it" (Matt. 10:39).

"Whoever would save his life will lose it; and whoever loses his life for my sake, he will save it" (Luke 9:24).

As a hope-bearer and healer, you can work for peace and justice in the community. Lots of pain and suffering could be alleviated if certain organizational and social structures were changed. Some persons, whom many call "losers," are losers not because of what they call "bad luck" but really losers because of "bad choices." However, many others are losers because of society's structures that discriminate against them. Their race, social class, or sex keep them tied to a certain position in society, and when illness, separation, aging, and death touch them, they are harder hit than others.

But you don't have to become a social analyst to be a

friend to the poor and disadvantaged. You can become a part of a healing mission, many of which are sponsored by religious groups in the community. Lose yourself in something greater than yourself and your sorrow, and the God who rescues you from the abyss of your worst anxieties will put your feet upon a rock and you shall stand.

As you and I part, may it be with a blessing:

"May God keep you safe until the word of your life is fully spoken" (Margaret Fuller).[12]

NOTES

1. John Bowlby, *Loss: Sadness and Depression,* vol. III, Attachment and Loss Series (New York: Basic Books, 1980), p. 7.

2. Erich Lindemann, *Beyond Grief: Studies in Crisis Intervention* (Northvale, N.J.: Jason Aronson, 1979), p. 61.

3. Colin Murray Parkes, *Bereavement: Studies of Grief in Adult Life* (Madison, Conn.: International Universities Press, 1972), p. 75.

4. Ibid., p. 94.

5. Paul E. Irion, *The Funeral and the Mourners* (Nashville: Abingdon Press, 1954), p. 73.

6. *Diagnostic and Statistical Manual of Mental Disorders,* 3rd ed. (Washington, D.C.: American Psychiatric Association, 1980), p. 333.

7. James Burns, "What It Means to Be Divorced," *Pastoral Psychology,* September 1958, pp. 45-52.

8. Robert Kegan, *The Evolving Self* (Cambridge, Mass.: Harvard University Press, 1983), pp. 159-60.

9. Judith Viorst, *Necessary Losses* (New York: Simon & Schuster, 1986), p. 288.

10. David Mace, *Abortion: The Agonizing Decision* (Nashville: Abingdon Press, 1972).

11. Karl Menninger, "Hope," *Bulletin of the Menninger Clinic,* 51, September 1987, p. 452.

12. Quoted in Nelle Morton, *The Journey Is Home* (Boston: Beacon Press, 1985), p. 30.